TRANSPARENT TRAUMA

START TRUSTING YOURSELF

KYLA ALLMOND

i

Kyla Allmond

Transparent Trauma

Kyla Allmond

TRANSPARENT TRAUMA

KYLA ALLMOND

Kyla Allmond

Transparent Trauma: Start Trusting Yourself

ISBN 978-0-578-88771-5

Copyright (c) 2021 by Kyla Allmond

Published by:

Noah's Ark Publishing Service
8549 Wilshire Blvd., Suite 1442
Beverly Hills, CA 90211
www.noahsarkpublishing.com

Editor: Rebekah J. Sawyer
Graphic Design: Christopher C. White
Interior Design: Kingdom Scribes

Kyla Allmond

TABLE OF CONTENTS

Kyla Allmond

Kyla Allmond

Dedication

To Samantha Slagle
Thank you for believing in me, even when I didn't believe in myself.

To all the trauma survivors,
Who have yet to discover the freedom, power, and strength in their own voice.

Kyla Allmond

Transparent Trauma

Kyla Allmond

Introduction

It was a sunny day in North Carolina. Mama was away visiting Granny who lived a couple hours away. Granny had had knee replacement surgery a few days before and Mama had gone to take care of her. It was the first time Dad, my sister Kendra, and I had the house to ourselves. I was super excited because Mama's mood was unpredictable and volatile at times, but Dad always knew how to calm her wrath. Dad was my favorite; he was calm and spoke very few words. Most importantly, he always saved me from Mama's temper. He and Mama had adopted Kendra and me, so he had to be a pretty decent person, right?

That day, Dad and I were on the couch in the living room watching *The Jetsons* on TV. I felt completely safe and relaxed. It was something we always did as a family, but this was the first time I got to spend one-on-one time with my Dad. The episode was just starting, and I was humming along to the theme song. Then I felt Dad grab my hand. I didn't think anything of it because he had held my hand plenty of times. It made me feel safe. This time it was a little different, though. He pulled my hand closer to him, and I felt a little weird. Then he slid my hand into his boxers. I began to feel nervous butterflies in my stomach and I yanked my hand back. He looked at me and softly said, "It's okay," and I believed him. He slid my hand back into his boxers, and his manhood was warm and throbbing. It was intriguing and confusing to me. It felt wrong, but Dad said it was okay.

At the tender age of nine, I was introduced to what would become my confusing relationship with men and sex. That incident was not my first encounter with "trauma," and certainly would not be the last. ***Transparent Trauma*** was birthed out of my own experiences, with the hope to empower those who have experienced trauma in their lives and restore their faith in humanity. After years of therapy and working on myself, I finally began to start trusting myself. I have come to the place in my healing process where the next step is to help heal others. Take this journey with me—from pain to healing—as I break down the walls of shame and expose the ugly truth behind my scars.

x

Kyla Allmond

CHAPTER ONE

The Night I Was Taken

I was born in Greene County, North Carolina, to Wendy Church and Billy Ellison. I was a whopping 8-pound 10-ounce baby. My mother wanted me to have a unique name and chose "Kyla Blair Church." She considered naming me "Kayla," but she decided to remove the extra "a" to make my name different. My name suits me as I've always been kind of different. I am my mother's first child, and my dad's youngest child and only daughter. Being the stubborn person I am, I was born two weeks past my due date via a C-section on October 31, 1990—I know, yes—on Halloween. I've heard that all my life. My maternal grandmother, Patricia Church, was the first to hold me. She said I stuck my hand out to wave before the doctor had a chance to pull me all the way out.

I have the distinction of being the first biracial child on both sides of my family. My mother is White and my father is African American. There was a lot of controversy behind my birth, especially on my mom's side; she dealt with a lot of judgment from her family. One of my aunts even said she'd rather be gay than be with a Black man. Ironically, that same aunt ended up with a biracial child. Eventually my mom's family did come around and accepted me.

I don't have any memories of my dad from the time I lived with my mom, most likely because he was always in and out of jail. I was six years old when he visited me for the first and only time, and that was at my grandparent's house. It was then I found out that his frequent incarceration was the reason why he hadn't been in my life. His visit was short-lived; we played a game of catch, talked a little, and he left. I was an adult the next time I saw him.

My mom made sure I knew some things about him, though. She said he was very handsome, about five feet nine inches tall, with a caramel complexion, and beautiful, curly hair he wore in waves. I get my hair texture from him. Mom said he treated her very kindly, and was a quiet, mild-mannered man. He just had a problem staying out of jail and staying clean from crack cocaine. His cycle of incarceration and drug use continued for the majority of my life. His longest bid around that time was for a rape he said he didn't commit. Speaking to him later in my 20s, he told me the story. Dad said he was nineteen years old and dating a seventeen-year-old White girl. He had a sexual relationship with this young girl,

12
The Night I was Taken

which was looked down on where they lived. When her parents found out about her relationship with him, the girl claimed he had raped her. Dad said she was more worried about her family knowing about her relationship with a young black man, than the life-long mark her accusation would have on his future. After his conviction, I think spending time in jail just became normal to him. Mom always said some people feel more comfortable in jail than in the "real world."

My mom must have moved on at some point, because when I was two weeks old, someone else stepped up as my father, Lester Sutton, my younger sister Kendra's father. Lester raised me as his; he never made a difference between Kendra and me even though she was the only biological child he shared with my mom. For years, everyone thought I was his daughter until I accidentally told the family the truth when we were reunited years later. Lester met my mom while he was serving time in prison; I'm not sure what he was in for or where he was imprisoned. Mom was pregnant with me, and as she was leaving the prison after visiting my dad, she saw Lester. He was a trustee there and cleaning the visitor's corridor. He said my mom approached him and gave him her number. He called her and the rest is history. Mom eventually broke up with

13

The Night I was Taken

my dad through a letter, and when Lester got released, he came to live with us. About three years later, my little sister Kendra was born.

There were some good times in our house. Lester used to make homemade fries for us. We loved when he cooked; his food was something everyone knew him for. However, Lester was cruel in some ways and found humor in others' pain. He would trick Kendra and me into believing hot sauce was ketchup and laugh when we cried from the heat burning our mouths. I also remember the time he whipped us both with a thick, leather belt after we had just gotten out the tub and were still wet. I don't know what we could have done at such young ages to deserve his abuse, but I do remember Mommy being angry and getting into an argument with him about it. He would also use my sister and me to mentally abuse Mom. He taught us to call her, "cracker-ass cracker," and he would egg us on to keep saying it. We were just chess pawns, not realizing the hurt we were inflicting on my mom.

My sister Kendra is beautiful. She has small, slanted eyes, beautiful thick, curly hair, and a beauty mark right by her nose. To her, I was her big sister, but to me I was her mom. Kendra and I had a love-hate relationship, at least on my end. She always adored and looked up to me, but to me she was a responsibility, and needed my protection. Mommy and Daddy got into fights often. Daddy would beat mommy badly and she would yell for me to take Kendra and hide. We would hide, but we could still hear her screams. I would hold my sister and tell her it was okay. I had to be strong for both of us. I couldn't let myself feel emotions; I wasn't allowed to. For the majority of my life, I didn't have that privilege. My sister wasn't strong enough to handle the fear on her own, so I had to be strong for her. Years later as an adult, I realized my animosity towards her started all the way back to when she was so little and innocent, and her safety was my responsibility. It wasn't her fault, but at four years old, I did not have the mental maturity to see it that way.

In addition to fighting often, Mommy and Daddy spent a lot of time in the bathroom. After they would come out, they would lie in bed for hours. We would call out to them, even climb in the bed with them, but our parents would not get up. On those occasions, I had to make sure Kendra was taken care of. One night she and I were both hungry, so we decided to make a cake. Our parents woke up to the smell of burning cake batter just in time to stop us from burning the house down. We got in so much trouble; however, we were the only ones who were being held responsible for making poor choices.

Kendra and I spent a lot of time doing things on our own. On hot, sunny days we would sit on the A/C unit on the patio outside our apartment with our friends from the neighborhood. Or we would explore the playhouse that my mom's brother, Uncle Danny, made for us. We lived in project housing in Lagrange, North Carolina, and basically, we spent a lot of time outside by ourselves. And it wasn't always safe there. Lots of accidents happened in that neighborhood, but the accident that scared

The Night I was Taken

us the most happened on the hill in front of our house, and it happened to me.

We always had a lot of toys because my mom would shoplift to support her drug habit. One day, I was riding one of those plastic tricycles that sat low to the ground, with a big wheel in the front. It was a popular 90s toy and mine was bright pink. I decided it was a good idea to ride down the steep hill that led to our doorway. I was going too fast, and suddenly I remember flipping over and over, rolling downhill, with my heart racing, until I finally landed on the pavement. I ended up with a big gash on the side of my head, and it was bleeding badly.

The neighbors ran out to see what had happened because I was screaming in pain. I remember them asking, "Where is this baby's mom? She is always leaving them out here." Someone sent one of their children to our house to get my mom. She ran down to me and I remember the embarrassed look she had while trying to comfort me. She knew it looked bad that she hadn't protected me. Mommy never protected me—hell, she couldn't even protect herself.

My mommy was beautiful. I look just like her. Everyone always told me how she kept Kendra and me dressed nicely and always had our hair done to perfection. Everyone says she was a good mom—the people who didn't live next to us, that is. My mom would babysit most of her friend's kids from time to time, but they didn't know she was a functioning addict. Her drug of choice? Crack cocaine. Her friends were shocked to find about her drug use when we were taken away from her.

18
The Night I was Taken

Most of the memories I have with Mommy and Lester are a blur. Only a few memories stand out—like the night we were taken. One day, Grandma came by to drive Mommy around to pay her bills. It was something she did every month. Grandma would take all of us, except Lester. We were always excited to see her and get out of the house, since we didn't have a car. When Grandma got there that day, the neighbors told her there was a situation going on with my mom. Grandma said my mom was high and completely out of her mind.

I'm not sure what my mom did, but there were a lot of angry people from the neighborhood threatening her about some money. Mom was waving a gun around in the air ready to defend herself. Grandma frantically grabbed Kendra and me. She had to get us out of the house with what we had on, which at the time was just underwear. I could hear the commotion, but it almost felt like I was outside of my own body; everything sounded muffled. I just remember red and blue lights flashing everywhere.

In the commotion, I don't remember where Grandma went, but at some point she wasn't there anymore. I remember the police coming and placing my sister and me in the backseat of the police car with the door slightly open. They wrapped a blanket around us; it

19

The Night I was Taken

wasn't cold outside, but I was shivering. I held my baby sister tightly. I had to be brave; I couldn't let her see that I was nervous, or she would get scared. I was only five years old at the time, and she was two; even though I was young myself, I had to comfort my sister, as I'd done so many times before.

While in the police car, I saw a familiar face coming around the door; it was my Aunt Lisa. She was my favorite aunt because she had such a warm spirit. I immediately felt relieved to see someone I knew. Thankfully, we went home with her that night. The next morning, we went to stay with Grandma and Grandpa. I thought we would be there for just one night, but we ended up staying with them for four years. That day was the last day I would ever live with my birth mother.

CHAPTER TWO

Emergency Care

Within every county of every state, you will find an organization responsible for the safety and welfare of the children within their district. In North Carolina, where I resided as a child, that entity is called Child Protective Services, commonly known as CPS. They only get involved when it is determined a child is being neglected, abused, or living in an unsafe environment. The goal is to keep children with their family and rehabilitate the parents if possible. In more serious situations, parents can lose their parental rights and lose custody of their children. The children will either be placed with relatives—if any are willing—or placed for adoption.

Mommy and Lester already had a paper trail with CPS prior to the night my sister and I were taken away from them. Our aunt Jeannine had previously called CPS on my parents a few times, and rightfully so. She was my mom's oldest sister and very worried about her nieces. Each time she called CPS, there was a concern about our safety. There had been several incidents of domestic violence, accusations of drug use, and neglect in our house.

Mommy and Lester's relationship was full of turmoil. Lester was very charismatic and liked by everyone; people always flocked around him. He had a big personality that drew you in and made you trust him; however, there was another side to him, as I said before. He had a habit of putting his hands on Mommy, especially when he was high. Mommy and Lester used crack cocaine together. They never used it in front of us, though. Mommy did a good job of hiding her drug habit from her children as much as she could. They would go into the bathroom together to use, and they did so often. When they went into the bathroom, Kendra and I would behave ourselves and watch TV with the promise of a toy if we let them "talk." Chaos always followed the "talks."

From what I know, there were only a few months between the first call to CPS and the last call that resulted in the removal of Kendra and me from the home. Surprisingly, we did not get removed because of our parents' drug use, although that was a major underlying factor. The main reason we were removed was because our house was deemed an unsafe environment due to the violence we witnessed on a regular basis— both verbal and physical. Mommy was scared of him, but she wasn't strong enough to leave, which ended up costing her—not only her children, but her sanity as well.

When CPS makes the decision to step in and remove children, they must find a temporary placement for them. For us, the best-case scenario was for us to go to family, and if we were lucky, we would be able to stay together. That was when my maternal grandma and grandpa stepped in. The social worker handling our CPS case reached out to our family to see who would be willing to take us. Ultimately, my grandparents made the decision not to take just one, but both of us. There were no legal custody arrangements made, but we were placed with them temporarily by the State.

To regain custody of us, the court gave Mom one year to get herself together. My mom was ordered to provide a safe place for us to live, to end the relationship with Lester, and to remain clean from drugs. That year came and went, and Mommy still did not have herself together. However, CPS was convinced and hopeful Mommy would get herself together and kept extending her more time—which she did not use wisely.

Transparent Trauma

Emergency Care

CHAPTER THREE

Safe Years

Grandma and my grandfather, Harold Church, lived in a little town called Snow Hill, North Carolina. There was not much to the town, and if you squint really hard at a map, you might be able to find it. My grandparents built a home together on thirteen acres of land. The house sat on a slope and there was a creek at the bottom. It took them six years to build the house with their own hands. It had a beautiful wraparound porch and looked like a log cabin. My favorite part of the house was the back porch. There was a view facing the creek and the whole side had humongous windows; it almost looked like the back of the house was completely made of glass. We spent a lot of time bird-watching on that porch.

Grandma had a green thumb and she always kept a big garden; she would plant a little bit of everything. Man, we ate a lot from that garden, and my sister and I loved to help her. We learned about pollination, insects, and even how to tell the difference between good and bad snakes. Grandma was always using nature as a learning experience. She was also an animal lover.

We always had a few dogs and cats hanging around the house. She would feed them all. Grandma taught me compassion through animals. Unfortunately, those beautiful glass windows always seemed to attract birds that couldn't tell that the windows weren't clear sky. The birds would hit the windows, and sometimes break their necks. We couldn't save those birds, so Grandma kept shoeboxes that we would use to bury them. We had to bury them deep enough so other animals wouldn't dig them up. Then there were the birds that had broken wings. Grandma would mend them and let them rest until they could fly again. We helped so many animals, even reptiles. I got my heart from her. She was so smart and caring, and even worked as a volunteer EMT for years, and she used a lot of those same skills to take care of us.

Grandpa worked at the West Company for years. He was the definition of a provider. He took care of Grandma, Kendra and me, and helped their five adult children whenever they needed something. Grandpa started at the West Company sweeping floors and worked his way up the ladder. He was a man of few words but meant what he said. Grandpa didn't hand out praise too often, so when he did it was a big deal. I remember the first time he told me he was proud of me; it meant the world to me. I felt like I had accomplished something huge. He loved woodworking and staying busy on his days off. I loved going into his workshop and watching him work. I can still remember the sounds of the machines running and the smell of sawdust settling on the wooden floors. There were scrap pieces of wood all over the floor, and I would get so excited about the possibilities of all the things I could make out of those little pieces of wood. He even showed me how to use his tools, even the ones he knew Grandma would be upset to know I was handling. Grandpa was always so patient, and he never made me feel like I was in the way. He taught me how to figure things out on my own by giving me the tools I needed to make what I envisioned, and stepping away to let me figure out the rest. This helped develop my creativity.

A favorite project I remember was building a birdhouse when I was about seven years old. Helping Grandma save all the little birds made me grow fond of them. So, one of the first things I wanted to build was a birdhouse to keep them safe. I sat in the shop all day trying to figure out the perfect pieces I needed to make the birdhouse. Grandpa let me fiddle around the shop and pick up little scraps of wood, steal his nails and his hammer, and whatever else I could get my hands on. When I was done, I had built an incredible birdhouse that still sits on my grandma's back porch some twenty years later. Grandpa helped me discover what my hands could do. Learning different skills exposed Kendra and me to a lot of fun adventures at Grandma and Grandpa's house.

We didn't really watch a lot of TV there. Grandma was funny about us sitting in front of TV all day. When we did watch TV, it was PBS. There weren't a lot of shows on PBS, but *Sesame Street* and *Arthur* were a couple of our favorites. Grandma was huge on education, so we had to read for an hour to earn TV time. Kendra and I used to complain about it all the time. But as time went on, I became quite the bookworm. I could get lost in a book and I nurtured my love for books and stories upstairs in my room. I won many reading awards in school, and in second grade, I read the most books in the school and won a limousine ride.

I didn't mind not watching TV because we did so many other things at our grandparents' house. It was not unusual to find us girls outside covered in mud by the creek, trying to catch minnows with handmade nets. Or you might find us in the garden trying to catch lizards and trying desperately to convince Grandpa to build a habitat for them, so we could keep them as pets.

Most of the time, we just rode our bikes around with bare feet. Grandma used to yell at us all the time about wearing shoes so we wouldn't cut our toes. We also spent a lot of time playing with our best friend Max who lived across the street. We had thirteen acres of land to explore, and boy, did we. We built forts, we were Indians dancing around a campfire, we were explorers, or we were just about anything a child's imagination could come up with.

And oh, did we travel. Grandma and Grandpa were Jehovah's Witnesses, and we traveled a lot. Not only for conventions, but just because Grandma and Grandpa loved to travel. We saw some amazing places in those four years. We stayed in beach houses and visited caverns in Georgia that we passed through in a glass-bottom boat. We traveled to so many states and went to tons of museums; Grandma made sure Kendra and I knew about our African American and Native American heritage. We climbed mountains together and even visited a Cabbage Patch nursery. I was a 90's baby, so visiting the place where Cabbage Patch dolls were "born" was a big deal!

Grandma always treated us with respect and dignity; that was the one thing I loved about her. And Grandpa was always so patient and willing to teach us. I learned about compassion, honesty, integrity, picking up someone else's slack with a smile on your face, loyalty, and sacrifice. I also learned practical things like responsibility, how to be nurturing, and resourceful, how to save money, and how to mend a broken wing.

CHAPTER FOUR

I Thought It Was Love

Eventually time ran out for my mom. CPS had given her plenty of opportunities to get herself together to regain custody of Kendra and me. The only things they required was for her to get clean, leave my sister's dad Lester behind, and secure a safe place for us to live. I had an undying loyalty to my mom. I knew she would do everything she had to do to get us back; I believed in her that much. I remember the times we would visit her in rehab, and the times she would just show up to my grandma's house and sneak and see us against the court's orders.

We would have supervised visits with Mom at the Social Services office, and I remember how weird it felt not to be able to leave with her. According to everyone else she was not a fit mother, but in my eyes, she was my mother, and she was a perfect mother. I remember the last visit we had together. My mom walked down the hall with a shaven head and stitches running down the side of her head. She had brought two huge coloring books for Kendra and me and on the inside she had written, "Mommy loves you." She told us some bad people had beaten her up badly and we cried. She reassured us she would be okay and promised us no one would hurt her again.

At that age, I was only worried about my mom, it never dawned on me she was not giving me what I needed. Grandma and Grandpa never gained legal custody of us even though we were placed with them by the Department of Social Services. Consequently, when Mom ran out of time to meet the court's stipulations, Social Services had already lined up families interested in adopting us. Grandma said everything happened so quickly; they were suddenly notified that Kendra and I were up for adoption, but they did not have an opportunity to take all the legal steps to gain custody of us. They were simply told it was time for us to go.

Thus, our journey to find a new family began. The first couple we met was a biracial couple. I don't remember their last names because we were with them very briefly, but I do remember the wife was Caucasian and named Wendy—the same name as my mother. The husband's name was Stephen. Wendy and Stephen had been married for some time and were unable to have children. We did not find out until later, but they had decided to adopt a child as a last-minute attempt to save their marriage. Ultimately that plan did not work. My grandma liked the idea that they were a biracial couple, and

I did too because I felt like we would fit in better; it would look more natural for my sister and me.

Things started off well in the beginning; they seemed like really nice people. Stephen worked and his wife stayed home with us. The process started with us visiting them every few weeks. That's the way Social Services set up the transition, so we could get acclimated to their home and comfortable with each other. The plan was for them to foster Kendra and me, then adopt if everything worked out. Kendra was a lot more receptive of the idea of having new parents. I wasn't. I was three years older than her; I loved my mommy, and I knew she loved me. I was still holding on to the hope she would come and get us, and I didn't want to betray her. Consequently, I didn't make it easy for Wendy and Stephen to love me. Kendra didn't understand because she was more open to love—it didn't matter where it came from. I felt like Kendra was betraying our mother and that created a lot of resentment in me towards her; it was then that I started bullying my sister.

I would pick with Kendra and she would tell on me. I would get angry and find sneaky ways to hurt her. Many of the things I did tore down my sister's self-esteem; I'm not proud of that today. I felt like I was losing the last person I had in my life. My sister was the last of my family and I didn't want to lose her to this new family. I don't

33
I Thought it was Love

remember what I did to my sister the last day we were at Wendy and Stephen's home, but it did not end well. I was having a rough day, and Kendra told Wendy I was being unkind, and as a result, I got angry, so angry Wendy could not calm me down. I was kicking and screaming, and I think my behavior just overwhelmed her. To contain me, Wendy bear-hugged me so tightly I almost passed out. She put me inside a closet and told me to sit there until Stephen got home from work. When Stephen got home and found me in the closet, he was irate with Wendy, and we were sent back home to Grandma and Grandpa. Kendra and I never returned after that.

Not long after that incident, we were sent to a new couple, Barbara and Dane Chapman. They were a Caucasian couple in their late 40s. They had been going through the adoption process for years after multiple failed pregnancies. Dane was a construction worker and Barbara stayed home and received disability due to a chronic back issue. Barbara wore the pants in their relationship; she was overbearing, direct, and somewhat annoying. Dane was soft-spoken and mild-mannered, and very private. Our first meeting with them was at Chuck E. Cheese; Grandma and Grandpa took us there to meet them. Of course, Kendra took to them right away. She was always open to letting new people in and it helped their case that we were meeting them at

I Thought it was Love

every child's favorite place. I wasn't impressed with them. They seemed nice enough, but I still had fresh memories of the last family.

I already knew they would like my sister better than me. Everyone always did. After the first visit, things progressed quickly from weekend visits to us eventually staying with them long term in a foster-to-adopt arrangement. Barbara and Dane seemed to be kind people before the adoption was finalized. They bought us brand-new fancy dresses and toys and let us eat whatever we wanted. Grandma never allowed that; we mainly ate out of the garden and didn't have sugar too often. For the first time in my life, I celebrated my birthday and Christmas. Grandma and Grandpa were Jehovah's Witnesses and those weren't holidays they observed. My mind was blown away from all the new things I experienced. Barbara and Dane's whole family was welcoming and kind and excited to meet Kendra and me. We were constantly reminded by them of how long Barbara and Dane had waited for us.

Time passed and the day came for Barbara and Dane to share the good news with us. I'll never forget that day. We were called to the living room, Barbara and Dana sat us down on the couch, and they asked us how we would feel if they adopted us. Of course, Kendra was immediately excited about the idea; however, I was not. I felt like we needed to wait on our mom.

35

I Thought it was Love

Barbara and Dane also told us we had the option to change our names and have our last names changed to theirs. They said they would not force us to be a part of the adoption; they would give us a choice. However, Barbara made sure to drill into our heads that our mother had chosen drugs and men over us. I didn't care about all that, I just wanted my mom. However, Kendra begged me to accept. I knew if my sister wanted to be adopted by them, I would have to also, so I told them I would agree because I didn't want to leave my sister. Kendra decided to change her name from "Kendra Danielle Sutton" to "Kendra Danielle Sabrina Chapman." I opted to keep my full name and just changed my name from "Kyla Blair Church" to "Kyla Blair Chapman." I still hate that last name to this day.

The adoption came and went, and all the excitement faded away. We had to go to church every Sunday and every Wednesday, and Barbara was very protective of us. We were not allowed to spend the night at anyone's home, including family. In school, she removed us from extracurricular activities and sex education classes. We were not allowed to attend dances or sleepovers. At the time I did not really understand why she was so controlling, but as I got older, all these things started to connect. We also moved a lot; it seemed like we moved every year.

That was our routine, until the day came when Barbara's mom, Granny, had to have knee replacement surgery. It was the day my innocence was stolen. I believe Dane waited for a perfect moment to have Kendra and me all to himself.

I found out later in life he had specifically asked to foster—and eventually adopt—little, Black girls for his own sick purpose. He slowly groomed me. I could never pinpoint when it started exactly, but I was the focus of his attention, and I didn't know why. My sister was just as beautiful as I was, plus she was nicer than me. However, for some reason, he was always focused on me. Dane would do things like smack my butt when I walked by him. I told Barbara it made me uncomfortable, but she wouldn't listen. She would tell me he meant nothing by it and I needed to stop complaining. As a result, I started to think that behavior was something normal for dads to do. Barbara would get angry at me, so she made Kendra her favorite. Because Barbara favored Kendra, I took my frustrations out on my little sister.

My sister endured a lot of emotional abuse from me as a child because I didn't have an outlet for my emotions. Whenever Barbara could blame something on me, she did. Barbara and Dane turned my sister and me against each other. Barbara had been raised by a military father and she would tell stories about how she was abused and told us the abuse she was inflicting on us was nothing like what she had endured. We were modern day slaves for her. She would mentally abuse us and keep us up for hours at night lecturing us, and if we dared fall asleep, she would whoop us. Barbara would punch both of us in the face or hit us with 1x2 pieces of wood, but it always seemed like her anger was more directed at me. Dane would stop her and tell her she was doing too much and would always intervene to save me. When his touching progressed to actual sex, I thought it was because he loved me; the molestation felt better to me than the beatings.

Because of my warped understanding of love, at the age of nine years old, I began looking forward to my alone time with him. Now that I'm older and I look back on that time, I can see exactly how sick and twisted it was. I'll never forget the first time he made me sit on top of him and I had an orgasm. I was so scared about what was happening to my body. He told me it was okay—that it was normal, that it was good—and I believed him. Even though in my mind it felt wrong, to my body it felt good, and that confused me. My grandpa never did those things to me, but I reasoned that maybe he didn't love me the way Dane loved me. Dane would tell me stories of other girls he had done those things to. He even told me about a thirteen-year-old he had had sex with on a motorcycle while in his 20s. He bragged about how much she had enjoyed it. In my young mind I thought, *"Well, if she thought it was okay, maybe it is okay."*

The sexual abuse by Dane continued for years. He made me hate Barbara by making me believe if she found out about it, she would hurt me even more than she already was hurting me. He told me she didn't understand how much he loved me. That was what I wanted to hear— someone thought I was special and wanted to protect me. I grew to love him in an unnatural way. Whenever he wanted, he could have his way with me. Whether it was sticking his toes between my vagina lips underneath the table while we were playing a family card game, or having me lie between him and Barbara while watching Cartoon Network in the morning so he could slip his fingers between my legs. Or spending time with me in the basement and using the garden tool handle to play with my privates. It became an exciting game I looked forward to—a secret we had just between us. It became normal, and because I was a child, I saw nothing wrong with it. Kendra resented me more and more, and every chance she got to blame me for something, she would, even if I didn't do it. Now that I'm older, I understand why.

As the years went on, the abuse by Barbara got worse. I hated Barbara because she always hurt me. Barbara would make me shovel gravel for the whole summer, wash my mouth out with soap, and make me scrub the floor with a toothbrush and a bar soap. One summer before my first year of high school, she dragged me down the steps by my hair and shaved all my hair off. I started high school with a fade. When people asked, she told them I wanted my hair cut like that. It was one of the most humiliating years of my life.

Barbara even started me on birth control at ten years old. I was having very heavy periods at the time, but I didn't understand why until I got older; she must have known her husband was having sex with me even then. She never let me attend sex education classes, so I missed critical information that would have explained what was going on in our house between Dane and me was wrong. However, I was completely clueless. In my mind, Barbara simply hated me. She was the villain and Dane was my knight in shining armor. He was the one who really loved me.

CHAPTER FIVE

Shame and Confusion

I will never forget the end of my seventh-grade year. I absolutely hated science and I had an incredibly old male science teacher. He was extremely strict and boring and I would always get in trouble in his class for talking. I had been labeled as a gifted student since second grade, so school had always been easy for me. I never really had to try hard to get good grades, but I always got in trouble for socializing because school wasn't a challenge and it bored me.

I had one Black friend in science class. Since I had been adopted by a Caucasian family, I always longed to be cool with kids who looked like me. She and I were the only two people of color in our class because we went to a school where the majority of the students were White. Her name was Diamond—she was tough, she was loud, and she was funny. Diamond spoke her mind, and nobody messed with her. She was bold and I wanted to be her friend so badly. I finally got my wish and we became friends. We sat next to each other and we would whisper and giggle during the whole class.

Diamond always wondered why I wasn't allowed to go to sex education class. I told her it was due to our religious beliefs. Diamond had a lot of questions for which I didn't have the answers, but we were friends that whole school year.

One day Diamond told me about a sleepover she was having and invited me to come. I told her I probably couldn't go because my mom didn't let me go anywhere. Diamond asked me why, and I didn't really know how to answer. At that point in my life, my spirit had been broken so badly by Barbara. I was scared to do or say anything wrong. I believed no matter where I was, that woman would know what I was doing, and I would be punished. She had that much mental control over me.

We changed the subject and Diamond started talking about her dad and the type of things she and her dad did together, and some of the activities they had planned for the sleepover. I sat and I listened, and the things she and her dad did together didn't sound anything like the things my dad and I did together. I sat and thought on it for a while and it really bothered me, so I asked her if her dad touched her private parts. I had to ask, because after listening to her, I had become confused; maybe what I felt was wrong at home really <u>was</u> wrong.

When I asked Diamond that question, her mouth dropped to the floor. She gasped deeply and said, "He's not supposed to do that!" I immediately felt ashamed, confused, and embarrassed, and so many other feelings I couldn't even put into words. She asked me had I told my mom, and I told her no, because my mom would be angry at me. Diamond told me I had to tell someone, or she would. I begged her not to tell anyone. I knew Barbara would hurt me; Dane had told me she would. Barbara hurt me for things I didn't do, what would she do to me for this? As I thought more about what Diamond said, I started to grow angry towards Dane because he had lied to me. He told me it was okay. He was the good one. How could he do this to me? I was confused.

Diamond told me she was going to tell, and she wasn't going to change her mind on that. I begged her all day not to. Eventually she promised me she wouldn't. I rode home on the bus that day scared for my life the whole way. I just knew Barbara was going to know I had told as soon as I got in the door, and she was going to hurt me in a way she'd never hurt me before. I sat on my seat and I didn't say anything to my sister. She asked me what was wrong, and I told her, "Nothing." All I could do was sit and think. That was the longest bus ride ever.

I walked in the house and Barbara greeted us like it was any other day. That didn't necessarily make me feel safe, because sometimes we would come home and she would act normally, then flip out on us. However, as the evening went on, she still acted like things were calm. I began to feel a little bit more relieved—then Dane came home.

As the night progressed, he came in my room as usual, pretending like we were playing some game alone. He shut the door and began to do what he would normally do. I was so angry at him, I told him, "This is wrong! You're not supposed to do this to me." He asked me, "Who told you that?" I told him about my friend at school, and he told me, "You know you better not tell Bar, because she will hurt you and I won't be able to protect you." I was so hurt and angry because his response showed me he knew what he was doing was wrong.

That night I went to my room and I cried. I told my sister what had been going on, because up until this point, Dane had only touched her, but he had not penetrated her. This was partly due to me; I would get jealous if I thought he was looking at her and I would come between them. Kendra was everybody's favorite. He was the only one who had made me their favorite. Kendra asked me if my friend had told anyone, and I told her I had begged her not to and I was confident she wouldn't say anything. That night Kendra and I made a plan that any time he tried to touch us, we would try to stop him, but we still wouldn't say anything to anyone.

I'll never forget the next time he tried to touch me. We had just come home from church and he came into my room and pushed me onto the bed. I was still in my church clothes, so when he lifted my dress up, I took the heels of my shoes and I kicked him right in the shoulders. Because he couldn't get anything from me, he went to my sister. She took a pushpin and poked it into the head of his penis. It was the first time my sister and I had worked together and been on the same page in years. We both felt betrayed and angry. We had decided Barbara would never believe us if we did tell on him unless we had proof to show her. However, Dane was manipulative; when Barbara saw the marks on his shoulder, he was able to convince her the marks came from an accident at work, and since he worked in construction, she believed him. Kendra and I were running out of options.

46
Shame and Confusion

CHAPTER SIX

Diamond Told

I entered science class that day like it was any other day. Class had just started and there was the usual hustle and bustle; everybody was laughing and playing, trying to get in last-minute conversations before the bell rang and it was time to take our seats. I sat in my normal seat next to Diamond, but she seemed a little off that day. I asked her what was wrong, but she didn't say much. So, I just sat in silence waiting for the lesson to begin. We were about ten minutes into the lesson when my name was called over the intercom and I was called to the office. My teacher gave me a hall pass and I walked to the front office. When I entered, I saw a lady sitting there with a folder in her hand, and my heart immediately stopped, and I knew—Diamond had told my secret.

I was taken to an empty classroom that had a table in it with about eight chairs around it, and a social worker sat me down. She explained to me she was there because one of my classmates had told her mother what I said about my father, and she wanted to have a conversation with me about it. I panicked; my heart was beating out of my chest. I felt nauseated, and more than anything, I was terrified about what Barbara would do to me. I was more worried about that than anything. The social worker reassured me anything we talked about would stay between us. I begged her to just leave it alone because I knew Barbara would hurt me. The social worker told me I was safe. She told me no one would hurt me and all she wanted to know was what was going on in our house so she could help me.

She was very persuasive, so I sat down with the social worker and explained everything to her. I felt like I was in that room for hours. When I finished explaining everything to her, she brought in a detective and I had to explain it all again. After a while, my sister was brought in and they talked to her as well. We were both crying and so overwhelmed, they let us have a bathroom break. I remember standing at the sink with my sister splashing cold water on our faces and my sister breaking down, crying and saying she hated whoever had told. She asked me, "How did they know?" I looked at my sister and told her it was me. She looked at me and asked, "Why would you do that?"

From that point on I knew I was on my own. Kendra ended up recanting her story, stating she didn't know about any inappropriate behavior by Dane. I continued with my story; I thought, *"I've already gone this far; I might as well finish the process."* Social Services promised me Barbara wouldn't be able to hurt me, so I sat with them and repeated my story over and over again. I had to explain every single detail, and they questioned me about whether he had penetrated me with his penis. It was one of the most uncomfortable things I've ever had to do. I was so young at the time, that even saying the word "penis" was uncomfortable. They made me go through every story over and over, and over again. I was emotionally exhausted, but I pushed through because they promised me I would not have to go back to the house, nor would Barbara be able to hurt me anymore.

However, that's not what happened. Barbara was very influential in our church and school; everyone loved her, but they didn't know the monster she was behind closed doors. She was also very manipulative. When she spoke with the social workers and begged them to send my sister and me home, promising she would make Dane leave the house, they believed her and sent me back into the arms of a monster. Barbara did make Dane go to a hotel room while the investigation continued. Forensics wanted me to go to a specialist, but Barbara would not allow them to do a rape kit on me. She told them that would be too traumatic for me, and since I had already been raped as a child, she wasn't going to put me through that. Those were all lies, but by law she had the right to refuse, and she did. So, they sent me home with her—the one person I was terrified of. The one person they promised they would protect me from. I would rather have been stuck with Dane. I learned from then on not to trust social workers.

Barbara could not wait to get her hands on me! When I returned home, she was waiting at the door and in my bones I could feel she was going to destroy me. I feared that woman more than I feared God. As a matter of fact, was there even a God? So many thoughts ran through my head. *"We went to church every Sunday and Wednesday. If there was a God, would he really let this happen to me? Where was this God I'd been learning about in Sunday school right now—the one I'd been praying to? I memorized all my Bible scriptures; I had been a good girl. Where was he now? Why did he let me go through all this? Why didn't He save me from her? They promised me. I can't trust anyone. Mommy didn't even come get me. I can't trust Kendra. I can't trust anybody but me. I've got to stand up for myself, protect myself."*

I made up my mind I was going to stand up to Barbara, and I was going to stick to the truth. I wasn't going to be scared even if no one was going to protect me. I had to protect myself. *"Shoot, was Barbara a god? How did she manage to get these people to believe her even after I told them she hurt me? Maybe I should fear her."*

As I walked through the door, she was right there waiting for me. I could feel the anger emitting from her body. I was so scared I could have peed on myself. She didn't ask any questions; she just looked at me and told me I was a liar. From that day on, she sat me up all night, every night, brainwashing me, telling me over and over I was a liar. She told me she'd better not hear me mention the abuse to anyone else again.

I repeatedly told her I was telling the truth. This routine continued for days; she'd keep me up all night and then I'd have to get up and go to school on little to no sleep. To add insult to injury, she would put me on the phone with Dane every night even though there was a "no contact order" against him. He said he still wanted to tell me he loved me every night, even though I had lied on him. He told me I needed to tell Barbara the abuse didn't happen or she wouldn't stop, because she didn't believe me.

The verbal torture continued up until two nights before the court date—and I finally broke from mental exhaustion. I gave in and said I lied so I could get some relief. Barbara told me I had to go to court and tell them I lied, or I would have to deal with her. And I believed her. I reasoned, *"The social worker hadn't helped me the first time; she actually made it worse. I shouldn't have said anything. I should have just kept quiet and let him touch me. Dane isn't here to save me from her. My situation is even worse than it was before."*

The court date arrived, and I got on the stand. I faced Barbara and the defense lawyer. He was drilling me like I had raped Dane. I felt like the only way to end the agony was to say I lied, like Barbara told me to say. If Dane went to jail, I would be stuck with her. I felt like no one could save me then. Therefore, I said I lied, and the case was dismissed. My social worker Mr. Justin ran up to me and asked, "Kyla, why did you do that? We had him! We had him!" Barbara quickly intervened and told him not to speak to me again. She ultimately got him fired for doing his job. She was evil like that.

After I recanted, Dane got to come back home, though it seemed he had never left, and I was labeled a liar. After being exonerated, He felt like he could do whatever he wanted, and he started messing with my sister. I told a teacher, Mrs. Carlson, about the abuse. She was my Civics teacher and I loved that subject because of her, and I felt I could trust her. I told her what had happened and she fought to reopen the case and get custody of me. Barbara was able to block her by citing double jeopardy laws and made me tell Mrs. Carlson I had lied so she would stay out of our business. Mrs. Carlson never looked at me the same after that and I still feel hurt about that today. I even tried to reach out to her as an adult, but I think she just didn't trust me anymore.

Barbara ruined a lot relationships and tarnished my credibility with a lot of people and family. She blocked my grandparents from having any alone time with me—even on the phone—so they never knew what was going on, even though she had promised them they would always be part of our lives. After Mrs. Carlson got involved, Barbara considered me a liability and got rid of me through a **C**hild **I**n **N**eed of **S**ervices (CHINS) petition through the courts. Children have to meet certain criteria to receive a CHINS petition. I was placed under the "stubborn child" category. No, seriously, that is a real category! Barbara convinced a judge I continued to falsely accuse her husband of raping me. Somehow, she won, and I was placed back into the foster care system and sent to Virginia's Home for Children, a group home located in Salem, Virginia. It was my first placement, but certainly not my last.

Transparent Trauma

Diamond Told

CHAPTER SEVEN

Moving Through the System

After the CHINS hearing, I was immediately sent away with the social worker. Barbara already had my bags packed when I got home; she was that ready for me to leave. The social worker picked me up and let me know I was going to a new placement at the Virginia's Home for Children, in Salem, Virginia. I remember being terrified the whole ride there; it was the first time I would be separated from my sister. While I was relieved to get away from Dane's and Barbara's abuse, I was also terrified of the unknown.

It was a long drive there and we passed a lot of mountains on the way. I didn't say much of anything for the whole ride; however, the social worker asked a few random questions, trying to make the ride less awkward. Finally, we came to a sign for the children's home. We turned off the main road and we went down a long, winding road. We pulled up to the children's home, which was actually a bunch of little houses spread out across a huge property. There were a lot of girls of all different ages outside walking across the campus. We pulled up to the administrative building, I grabbed my belongings, and I went inside. They sat me down at a desk with a lady who asked me a ton of questions. I don't remember the questions she asked, but I remember feeling angry when I heard all the rules. In fact, I was angry about everything.

I was angry I had been coerced into recanting my accusations against Dane. I was angry at Barbara for blaming me for what her husband had done. I was angry that I was being punished for being a victim. And I was even angrier at my sister who had turned her back on me and got to stay behind. That was the day I discovered I was angry at the world—and at God.

After the conversation with the lady in the front office, I was taken to a cottage and showed my room. I was introduced to about five girls and the staff who supervised the cottage. All the girls ran up to me and were excited to meet someone new, but I wasn't in the mood to get to know anybody. I had a lot of confusing feelings I needed to process, and it was my first time being away from Barbara.

I had never been allowed to have my own mind or make my own choices or even have privacy. As I unpacked my things, one by one the girls came in and asked me different questions. I told them I was there because my adopted dad had raped me. I told the truth about myself not really understanding how foster care worked; the same ones who asked questions out of concern could turn around and use that information to try to hurt you and make you mad. I didn't want to tell anyone I was a willing participant with Dane; I was too ashamed. It wasn't until I had therapy later did I understand I had been raped—it was not my fault. I was not old enough to know what I wanted, and Dane took advantage of me. He had groomed me for years. I was a victim, not a participant.

I was overwhelmed by all the things I saw in the group home. There were so many girls there. Some had been in the system since they were four or five years old and some of the girls had serious mental health and behavioral issues. I only lasted at that group home for three weeks. Once I got around the other girls and saw their behavior and how they did whatever they wanted, I was intrigued. Barbara had always controlled me, but I was able to see another side and that I could do what I wanted—so I did. I learned how to misbehave there. I learned I could say what I wanted, and the staff couldn't hurt me, so I took full advantage of them and the situation.

Unfortunately, I also learned about cutting and self-harm there. The girl in the room next to mine would cut herself, not with the intent of killing herself, but to relieve pain. It was something I had never considered as an option, so I tried it. I just wanted to see what it felt like. She had convinced me to do it and I liked it. I felt like I was in control. That's how the enemy works—he makes things look interesting, and he convinces you to do those things. He seeks you out in your lowest moments. Once I got entangled with her, things went downhill quickly within a matter of weeks. The group home staff decided they were unable to handle me. I had finally gotten a taste of freedom and I went from being completely submissive to out-of-control. It made me feel powerful; for first time in my life, no one could tell me what to do. However, at fourteen years old, I had no idea about what life was truly about and I didn't have anyone to teach me, so I did whatever I wanted to do.

My next placement was at the Pines Treatment Center in Norfolk, Virginia. "The Pines," as we called it for short, was a treatment center for mentally ill and out-of-control children. It was terribly similar to a children's prison. We had a canteen, dining hall, recreational time, even shower time—a schedule for everything. Every single door had magnetic locks. There were even isolation rooms that only had a bed and mattress in them. The beds had bolts on the side to connect restraints to hold a child by his or her ankles and wrists. Those rooms were used when a child was out of control and needed to be restrained. The child would be strapped to the bed, and if necessary, given a shot from the nurse to calm him or her down. The building was huge and had a school, a cafeteria, a gym, vending machines, and pay phones you could use if your family sent you money.

There were different units in the building, created to separate the children into groups according to their behavioral issue or mental health status. The boys and girls were always separated unless they had a co-ed event, which only happened once in a blue moon and were heavily monitored. You had to earn the privilege to attend. I never earned that privilege. As a result, I rarely had any interaction with males until I got out of foster care, ultimately creating issues later because I did not know how to interact with men in a healthy way. My only experiences involved men sexualizing me, which in turn made me feel like any man who talked to me just wanted me for sex.

As soon as I got to The Pines, I had to meet with the clinical team. They wanted to know each child's history and diagnosis immediately, often just for insurance purposes. Prior to being placed at The Pines, I had never had behavioral issues, not even in school. I don't quite remember what diagnosis I was given at first, but during my years in foster care, I was diagnosed with almost every disorder at some point in time. I went through many years of receiving wrongly prescribed medications, only to find out as an adult I was actually dealing with post-traumatic stress disorder (PTSD), a disorder which occurs after a person has experienced an tremendous amount of trauma. You can treat the symptoms of PTSD—like anxiety—with minimal medication, but it's most successfully managed with therapy. However, because treatment facilities thrive on billing and documentation, ensuring that insurance companies will pay, they push medication and diagnoses for children. Unfortunately, as a result, many times if you show four out of ten signs of a particular diagnosis, you will be labeled with that diagnosis.

After my meeting with the clinical team, I was placed in a unit with about twelve other girls, two to a room. You couldn't pick which girl you roomed with; nine times out of ten, you wouldn't get along with the girl you were paired with, but you had to make it work. I learned very quickly how to get along with people. There were girls in my unit who had serious issues and dangerous backgrounds, like teen pregnancy, drug abuse, and assault charges. Some had just gotten out of juvenile detention, or had serious mental health conditions like schizophrenia. I was in absolute culture shock—I was a country girl from North Carolina who had never even been in a fight. Although I had suffered abuse at home, I saw things in that facility I never thought were even possible. A few incidents I witnessed will always stick with me and many still haunt me today. I can't count the number of times I had to untie shoestrings from around the necks of girls who had attempted to hang themselves. Other terrible things I saw were girls shoving pieces of plastic into their arms, slamming their heads onto the side of A/C units, snorting medication, and making shanks.

The Pines was also the first place where I got into a fight. There was a girl in my unit who would bully me every other day, and I would just let her hit me. My grandma had always taught me to turn the other cheek, so I did. The other girls in the unit hyped me up and told me I needed to fight her or she was going to keep bullying me. They told me I shouldn't be a punk. To prepare me to fight, they gave me Vaseline to rub on my face to protect my skin, a scarf to tie my hair up, and a pair of Timberland boots.

That day I sat at the same table where she would come beat me up every other day, and the girls on the unit were playing the song, "Knuck If You Buck." I was high on adrenaline and scared I was going to be embarrassed, but I was also a little excited to do something so out-of-control. Just like clockwork, my bully came up and hit me upside my head. However, that day I fought back and drove her up and down the hallway—she never messed with me again. That was the day I learned I could fight.

After my first fight, I began picking on other girls and instigating fights with them. I had a mouth on me, and my hands matched. For once in my life, I felt powerful—no one could hurt me. I became destructive too; I didn't care who got hurt, even if it was the staff. I began to incite riots and make plans to break out. The girls were afraid of me and did what I said. Eventually I got kicked out of that campus as well. They had a second campus for aggressive girls located in Portsmouth, Virginia and I was sent there.

Since I had caused so much trouble at the Norfolk campus, they thought the Portsmouth campus would be better equipped to handle me. The Portsmouth campus had a whole different breed of girls. They were rough and tough, and most of the girls were from areas like New York City and Maryland. When I first got there, I was an underdog, but just like my experience at the previous campus, I quickly climbed to the top by fighting.

I had to go to therapy every week and I hated it. Once again, I was put on medication, but the number had grown to fourteen. To this day, I'm not sure of the long-term effects they may have had on me, but now knowing my diagnosis as an adult, I know many of the medications I was prescribed were unnecessary. I hated everybody and everything there. I was sixteen years old and had yet to be around boys, so I started experimenting with girls. I would only kiss them; I never was willing to go any further. It was the normal thing to do there, and most of the girls experimented as well. We didn't have contact with any males and I think we all just desired to feel loved. I don't consider myself to be homosexual. In fact, as an adult, I have no sexual interest in women at all. That experimentation was a part of my past, and unfortunately, it is a real part of foster care and it happens often when children of the same sex are isolated from the opposite sex for years at a time.

I hated it at the campus in Portsmouth and felt abandoned. Barbara and Dane just dropped off the face of the earth. They called every once in a while, but each time they would upset me and I would cuss them out because I knew they couldn't touch me. Whenever I would get upset like that, I was just validating Barbara and Dane's allegations that I had had a mental breakdown. I refused visitation with them and in return they never sent me money for the phone or to get food from the canteen. On holidays, the families of the other kids would send gifts and care packages, and a lot of times I would be the only one who didn't get anything.

To compensate, I learned how to play spades well to win snacks. Spades is a game of strategy and memory, a game of manipulation; I learned a lot of skills on how to survive through playing spades. It was one of my favorite games to play and I was very good at it.

I had a monthly treatment meeting with the clinical staff to review my treatment plan. They would sit me down and look over my diagnosis and medications and come up with a new plan to determine how long I had to stay in the treatment center. At every meeting they had new information to add. Of course, they did; I was being triggered by Barbara and Dane's phone calls, then forced to cohabit with children who were violent. I had to learn to be violent to survive. On top of all that, I was simply angry for being locked up because someone raped me.

Consequently, my treatment meetings never went well; the staff would compile all my behaviors to justify to the insurance company why I needed to stay longer. My first treatment plan was projected to last six to nine months. By the time I had my last treatment plan meeting, the term had been extended to three to four years. Every time I left those meetings, I would be furious. I would go back to my unit and just start acting out because I didn't see the point in even trying. No matter what I did—even if it was exhibiting normal angry emotions—no one understood me, no one cared about me, and I felt I was never going to get out of that place. The only way you could be released from The Pines was if you were admitted to a psychiatric hospital. You would have to voluntarily sign yourself out of the treatment center and sign yourself into the psychiatric hospital. Some of the girls would make minor cuts on themselves just to get sent to the psychiatric hospital. The hospital was a better facility; the staff was nicer and the food was better.

I was also a good problem solver. I knew the only way I was going to get out of there was if I broke out and ran away or if I figured out a way to get released. So, I developed a plan to get out of The Pines. The first time I went to the psychiatric hospital, I cut myself to get admitted. They were small cuts because I really didn't want to hurt myself. I had to hold my breath while I made the cuts—hell, they hurt. My first visit in the psychiatric hospital was very enjoyable. I tried to act out there and fight and I was caught with a needle early on. It was the first time I realized that outside of the treatment center, the way I handled things was the right way. Again, these were all learned behaviors. When my time was up, I had to sign myself out of the psychiatric hospital. Unlike my first visit to the treatment center, they allowed me to voluntarily sign myself in.

After a couple months, I learned how the paperwork was processed, and I made a plan to go back to the psychiatric hospital, but I wasn't going to go back to The Pines. I played out the same scenario as before and went to the psychiatric hospital. When it was time to go, I signed myself out. When they took me back to the lobby of The Pines treatment center, they asked me to voluntarily sign myself back in, and I refused.

Usually, if it was a weekday and a child refused to sign in, the staff would call the courts and the courts could file a CHINS petition and force the child to go into the facility. However, I had been released on a Friday evening, and the courts were closed, and they couldn't file the petition—I had forced their hands. The staff was frustrated with me because they knew I had outsmarted them and there was nothing they could do to make me go back into The Pines. I had finally done it; I had outsmarted them and was leaving that terrible place.

Most of the girls who left The Pines didn't leave until they were eighteen or nineteen years old, and then they were put into group homes for the mentally ill as adults. Even the good girls ended up in a worse situation. I thank God every day that He gave me the knowledge to escape that place. Years later the government shut down The Pines down due to the horrific things the children experienced there.

My social worker was contacted and Social Services had to place me in an emergency foster care home; there was no other option for them. I was so excited because I went from being told I would not be released out of that prison for three years, to going to a regular house. My social worker came and picked me up, and we took a long drive to Martinsville, Virginia. In a three-month-period, I was placed into several different foster homes with single women and even a group home. I didn't last long in any of those placements. Unfortunately, I had been conditioned to fight and act aggressively due to my experiences in treatment. When it was time to reenter the real world, I had no problem-solving skills, at least not the healthy kind.

To those trying to place me in foster and group homes, and the foster parents I was sent to, I acted all the way crazy, out of control, mentally ill, and dangerous. At the time, I was all those things, but honestly, I was just a misguided little girl who had to fight to survive, and I didn't know how to turn off my survival mode mentality. No one had taken the time to get to know me; they had only taken the time to judge me. After being discharged from my third placement in the Martinsville area, the state of Virginia decided there were no other placements willing to accept me, and The Pines treatment center was not willing to take me back because I had outsmarted them. As a result, I was deemed a "hard placement."

The next step was to send me to Mountain Youth Academy in Mountain City, Tennessee. It was a treatment center out in the middle of nowhere. It was set up very similarly to the Pines Treatment Center, but they accepted children who were hard placements from other facilities. I remember driving up the long, winding road and wondering when the road would end. We passed tons of trees and forests—it was miles away from any houses. It seemed like the facility was on its own island. Looking out the window I thought, *"No way am I going to run away from here. I might get lost in the woods, get eaten by a wolf, and die."*

I had a bad attitude when I arrived because I thought I had left the treatment centers behind me. When I first walked in, everyone was nice and cheerful. I didn't want them to be nice to me. The staff at the other treatment centers were nice to me at first, and then they would turn. However, the staff was so nice to me, I felt like I had to be nice as well. I got a little bit excited and I showed them all the blankets I learned how to crochet in my art class and they were amazed. I didn't know how to take all the positive attention. My good behavior lasted about three weeks, however, which I later found out was what they called the "honeymoon period." Whenever a new student arrived and adjusting to the new environment, they don't show disruptive behaviors at first, which was why they called it the "honeymoon period." For about three weeks, I was well-behaved. However, just as it happened at the other facilities, after my initial excitement wore off, a girl started messing with me, and I got right back into the old cycle. I started fighting and being destructive again. However, unlike times in the past, the staff greatly reduced—not increased—my medication dosages and I was assigned to a therapist.

I was only at Mountain Youth Academy for about a year, but it was the place where I made my turnaround thanks to the staff there. Don't get me wrong, although there were a lot of great staff members there, there were a few bad ones too, like the ones who loved when the call for "all available staff" was given, so they could restrain you. However, I loved when "all available staff" was called to an incident; it was exciting to me and made me feel like I could fight anybody—which I did. I would fight eight staffers at a time just because.

Then there were times when I really wanted to be loved and there were staff there who would sit up late at night and talk to me and hug me and bring me things they weren't supposed to. Those were the staff who made the difference in my life. I was seventeen years old when I got there, and I finished my GED there. Because I had moved around so much and attended so many different schools, it was either get my GED or be in high school for four more years. I chose to do my GED. I didn't even study and I passed the first time I took the test.

After years of fighting the system and the staff at all the treatment centers I had been assigned to, I finally gave up because the people at Mountain Youth Academy were so kind to me and wouldn't give up on me. I finally realized the only way I was going to get out of that place was to actually work the program. I wanted them to send me away; I wanted them to give up. I didn't want anyone to love me. I felt God didn't love me or else He wouldn't have let me be placed there.

When people loved me, it always seemed like they ended up hurting me. However, after I stopped fighting, I ended up working the program, and I was successful. When it was time to graduate, I moved to a step-down placement. The next step was to move to an independent living home, which would allow me to finally transition into the world as an independent person. I remember the day it was time for me to leave. Everyone cried; I cried too. I still have pictures of me with all the staff members. I was a success story. I came in as a girl no other facility wanted and left as a different person.

After I left there, I was sent to the Jackson-Feild Homes for Girls in Jarratt, Virginia, which was a group home/independent living program. I got my first job there working in the cafeteria with a Christian woman named Miss Kindred, whom I affectionately called "Ma," and with an older lady everyone called "Grandma."

They played gospel music and taught me how to run the kitchen; I loved being in the cafeteria with them. It was the first time I had a woman nurture me. Mrs. Kindred was mild-mannered; she didn't curse, and she would teach me about God, no matter how much I didn't want to hear about Him. She remained the same no matter what, and that made me desire to get to know this God she talked about; she had to have been the sweetest person I'd ever met. I also attended the church services a local pastor held at the campus, and I even joined the praise team. I finally started believing in God again.

Although I had a job in the cafeteria and was singing with the praise team, I was also eighteen years old and really interested in sex. I hadn't been allowed the freedom to be around guys, so I chose to have sex for the first time in a car in the college parking. The girls in the group home hyped me up to do it because I'd never had sex by my choice before. And I felt like I was grown. It lasted about two minutes and I felt like crap afterwards. The guy didn't even talk to me anymore after it happened, which confirmed to me I was only good for sex to men. The second time I had sex, I snuck a twenty-eight-year-old guy in the window of my group home. He was handsome and I thought he really liked me.

I didn't have much experience with guys, even though I was eighteen years old, so I naively thought the fact he came all the way out there to meet me meant he thought I was special. He came and did what he did and left, and I ended up with an STD. I was hurting afterwards and found out I had chlamydia. I remember going to the nurse to get treated, thinking I was pregnant; I didn't know how impregnation happened back then. Once again, I was devastated and realized I was just a sex object for men. After my first two sexual experiences, I didn't have sex for a long time.

I had very few bad incidents at the Jackson-Feild Homes for Girls. I was maturing and learning to control myself. However, after about nine months there, I was told the funding for my placement was no longer available and my social worker was going to move me. I was devastated; it was one place I did not want to leave. Thankfully, the staff came together and told my social worker they could use some surplus funding they had to sponsor me for the rest of my placement. I had done so well in the program, they didn't want me to leave. So, instead of being shipped to a new place, I was sent to the Eleventh House, their independent transitional house in Richmond, Virginia. Honestly, I hated the Eleventh House. I wanted to go to back to the main campus, but I didn't have a choice. I was just grateful they had at least bought me more time with them so I wouldn't have to go to another facility.

At the Eleventh House, I was able to start my first job in the real world working at Hardees. The job only lasted about three weeks. I still had so much emotional growth to accomplish. Being in foster care had stunted my ability to adapt to "normal," real-life situations, but I was able to further my academic studies. I began my second semester of college at the Eleventh House. I could not figure out my major, so I mainly took general studies classes. My load was a bit heavy, but I did well. I took fifteen credit hours, with a 3.8 grade point average; however, I never finished college. I could not decide what I wanted to study or what I wanted to pursue as a career. In the end, I got bored with college, just like I did in grade school. I met a lot of good people through Jackson-Feild Homes for Girls and the Eleventh House, many of whom I remain in contact with even to this day.

I got provoked a lot there too, though I'm not sure why; I attributed it to the fact I was really nice and the kids smelled weakness. I worked hard to control my anger before I got there, but there was one incident which made me realize if I didn't control my anger, I was going to die or I was going to hurt someone else and up in jail. There was a staff member who provoked me a lot and I knew if I put my hands on her, I was going to go to jail and get kicked out. I didn't want that to happen, so when she provoked me one day, I punched a window instead of punching her, not thinking the window was going to hurt me. I know it sounds stupid, but that was the reasoning of a teenager.

When I pulled my hand out of the window, blood was spurting out of my arm like a water faucet. I remember sitting down and one of the girls slapping me in the face to wake me up because I had passed out from all the blood loss. The next thing I remember was waking up in the ambulance and then waking up again in the hospital. The glass had severed a main artery completely in half and it was irreparable, so they had to tie off the artery.

I remember sitting on the hospital bed, angry because the nurses kept asking me if I had tried to kill myself. That was not even on my mind. It was ironic; the one time I tried to use self-control, I ended up seriously hurting myself. I knew then I had more work to do on myself. I still hated it there, but I started taking classes and enrolled in a nine-month program to be a certified nursing assistant at the adult development career center in Richmond, Virginia. It was a great program, and I was the salutatorian of my class.

During my stay there I met a lady named Anna Hembrick. She was a registered nurse and my instructor. Every day we talked, she wanted to know a little bit more about me and why I hated being there. She learned how I was provoked and how I didn't feel like I could stay on the good track there. She was very understanding and kind. Before my stay at the Eleventh House was over, I went to my social worker and asked if it was possible for me to move in with Anna Hembrick and her family until the funding became available for me to get my own apartment.

My social worker allowed her to do it, and I moved in with Anna and her husband, and their children. Looking back, I sometimes tell her she was absolutely crazy to bring an eighteen-year-old from a group home into her own home, but God works in mysterious ways. They embraced me and their family embraced me. They did so much for me, like including me in their holiday celebrations, and even helping me completely furnish my first place. She took me in like I was family and truly restored my faith in people. I'm still in contact with her to this day. She was just one of the people I've met along the way who've come out of nowhere to love me more than my own family did. I just had to be willing to let them love me.

I was able to transition to my own apartment about three months later and I linked up with a girl who was in foster care with me previously. She happened to be pregnant, and I let her move in with me, which was against the rules. I had saved up a little money from my job at

Hardees, and my social worker matched my savings and I was able to buy a little Mazda. I had no idea what to do with all the freedom I had, so I ran with it. I had a car and I fell in love with the streets.

It was exciting; it was unpredictable; it was fun. Having my own apartment only lasted for a couple months. I had so many people running in and out of my apartment and I pretty much did whatever I wanted to do. My social worker gave me an ultimatum: put my roommate out or lose my apartment. I chose to lose my apartment. That was a dumb decision, but once again, God looked out for me and one of my friend's mom took me in for a little while.

I was blessed with another apartment about a month later. I stayed in that apartment for a couple weeks and then got into a bad car accident. Things were rough for me, but it was around the same time I met my husband. After I had the accident, I wasn't able to work for a while, and my future husband's sister and her family took me in. That's a whole other story for another time.

CHAPTER EIGHT

Drug Train to Nowhere

Now that I'm a lot older and I look back on the laundry list of pharmaceutical drugs I was on from the age of fourteen to eighteen, I am appalled. Being pushed through the system, I saw a lot of messed up things and realized how much money impacts the way children are treated in foster care. A significant amount of the funding sources and insurance companies require children in foster care to see a psychiatrist or have a mental, emotional, or psychological diagnosis to provide funds or services. There is a lot of money in mental health. Unfortunately, even when a child—or a client in general—does not fit the criteria for treatment, administrators may adjust diagnoses or paperwork to make that child or client fit the criteria. The bottom line is this: the mental health field is a business.

I have been on about sixteen different medications since the age of fourteen. At one point I was taking eight pills in the morning, and eight pills in the evening. A lot of the girls placed with me were on the same medications and they would either sell or trade their pills, or just not take them at all. We knew we were being force-fed pills. You could refuse your medication; they did give you an option. However, if you didn't take your medication, then you would be found non-compliant with your treatment plan, and your stay would be extended. You either had to model good behavior without the pills or just go ahead and suck it up and take them. Then they would tell us we were doing great because we were zombies from the medication; we weren't even capable of making decisions for ourselves. We were manageable on the pills, just like tranquilized animals.

At one point, the clinical staff had me on lithium and tried to diagnose me as bipolar. The lithium caused me to have seizures and I was taken off it immediately. Over the years I felt like a lab rat, and no medication ever worked. I realized later the medication didn't work because I had been misdiagnosed. The only thing I needed was a good therapist, someone to understand the real me behind all the anger and violence, who would take the time to get to know me, work with me, and be patient with me. Unfortunately, that didn't happen. I didn't have a choice; I was forced to take medication.

Now as an adult I do take anxiety medication, but I'm only diagnosed with prismatic stress disorder for which I go to therapy weekly—by choice. It took me a long time to conclude it was okay to take these steps because I had such mistrust towards medication and therapy. I'm not sure what the long-term psychological effects of taking all those different medications may have had on me or the other girls. What I do know is most of us were forced on them and hated taking them. As a result, as adults, most of us refuse to take medication, even when we need it.

It really is a shame how the mental health field works. There are a few good people in the field who care about their jobs and really want to make a difference. However, the people who treat clients like animals who need to be tamed are the ones who give those in the mental health field a bad reputation. Thankfully, I had great counselor who changed my whole opinion about mental health workers; her name was Samantha.

CHAPTER NINE

Samantha

I first met Samantha when I was assigned to her caseload at Mountain Youth Academy. I had already decided therapy was not for me and made up my mind I was not going to like her. I felt the staff just wanted me to sit there and talk to her for billing purposes. She was a petite, White lady with reddish-brown hair and a pretty smile. She was soft-spoken and very patient, but I didn't care about any of that. She was just being nice because it was her job. In one of our first sessions, I told her I was only there because I had to be. I had been going to therapy for years and I didn't see the point; it never helped and no one ever listened to me. I even told her all the bad things I had done. I didn't really want to change; being aggressive and fighting everyone protected my feelings. I was impenetrable. I remember her telling me I didn't have to say anything; all I had to do was sit there for an hour because it was required.

Samantha was so nice; I couldn't stand her. She seemed weak to me. Having been in different treatment facilities and group homes for so many years, I could smell weakness in someone—at least I thought I could. With my insight, I went from being a victim to being a bully. I would pick with Sam every chance I got. I would throw stuff, cuss her out, and even make her cry, but that lady would not go anywhere. She opened each session with a smile and a kind word. No matter how nasty I was, she remained calm. Oh, it made me hate her. I didn't understand why I couldn't get a reaction out of her, nor did I understand why she wouldn't go away and give up.

I remember the day that changed my life forever and ended up being the first day of the rest of my life. I don't quite remember exactly what led up to it, but I remember I was angry and yelling in Sam's office and I asked her, *"Why the fu** won't you go somewhere? Why can't you just leave me alone? I want another therapist!"* She looked at me and yelled back, *"I'm not going anywhere because that's what you want me to do! You're so scared, you don't want me to care about you, so you're trying to push me away. There is nothing wrong with you. You are just someone who's been through a lot of fu**ed up stuff and you're angry...and I'm not giving up on you!"*

I broke down that day. I felt horrible. She was the first person who hadn't given up on me and I had treated her so badly, basically treating her the way others had treated me. My head was so messed up I didn't even know what love looked like and it had been in front of me the whole time. She broke through a wall with me that day; she gained my trust and made me believe people could love me again. Most importantly, she made me believe in myself again. How could I give up if someone wasn't giving up on me?

After that day, I worked hard in therapy. I made every session and I was a willing participant. Samantha helped me work through so many things and helped me recognize I had in fact been raped and was not a willing participant. She made me realize I wasn't crazy or out of control; I was a person who had been let down and abused my whole life. I was a survivor. I was a real-life soldier fighting every day, and I didn't have to fight anymore. I changed—she helped change me. She helped me forgive myself and others. Thanks, Sam.

Samantha

Chapter ten

Plans to Kill

It was 2012. My husband and I had been married about six months and had a one-year-old daughter. We were lying in bed, dead asleep. I got a phone call about two o'clock in the morning from my sister Kendra, and she was frantic. We had just reconnected not too long before this. She—and Barbara—were on the line. They both were crying and apologizing to me. My sister told me she had confronted Dane about what he had done to me, because she had been told the story that I had lied for years. But she believed I was telling the truth. I didn't know how to feel about what she said because Kendra was there when it was happening and all of a sudden she was saying <u>now</u> she believed me. Maybe she was too young when it happened and had forgotten. Maybe they had brainwashed her.

Either way, she and Barbara called to let me know Dane had finally admitted what happened. He told them he had sexual relations with me, but if anyone asked, they didn't have to know. However, he told them he did <u>not</u> rape me. He said I wanted it and I didn't stop him. Of course I didn't stop him. Why the hell would I have tried to stop him? He had made me feel like it was okay! Dane's "confession" sucker-punched me. I finally had some kind of closure, but he still believed he had done nothing wrong. Barbara sat on the phone explaining herself and crying, saying she'd gone back and forth and still wondered if it had really happened or not. She did say she was sorry for what had happened to me, and everything I had gone through. I let out a sigh of relief to know I had finally been vindicated. For years people had accused me of lying about that man. Finally, he had told the truth out of his own mouth. We called my grandmother in the middle of the night to tell her about Dane's confession and Barbara apologized to her as well.

I remember that night ending with me breaking down; I was so relieved the truth was out. I got a call from my sister the next day and she was angry. She told me Barbara had told Dane if he went to therapy, she would stay with him. Kendra also told me she and Barbara were moving to Florida, just the two of them. She and Barbara drove down to Florida and were staying in a hotel room. Kendra and I both talked to Barbara about filing charges against Dane again, with Kendra and Barbara supporting me. However, I was unable to do so due to double jeopardy laws. Plus, Barbara suddenly got cold feet. She said she did not remember him <u>actually</u> admitting anything and she did not want to get involved. That night she left Kendra at the hotel and drove back to North Carolina, leaving my sister stranded in Florida with no money. My grandfather sent money to my sister to catch a Greyhound bus to the home I shared with my husband.

I was enraged. That woman had watched me go through so much. I finally had a chance to make it right, and after everything she had done to mess up my life, she had turned around and abandoned my little sister. I wanted to hurt her and Dane. I wanted them to suffer the way I had suffered. Kendra and I sat down and thought of every possible way we could make them suffer slowly. I didn't want to make it easy; I wanted it to be tortuous and painful, the same way my whole life had been because of them. Honestly, I wanted to cut off his penis and let him bleed to death slowly and I wanted her to watch just like she watched him do what he did to me. He was getting away with it again and I was angry because she was helping him again.

I wanted to take him out so he could never abuse another little girl. I hated him; I hated her. What kind of desperate woman, who knew her husband not only cheated but was also a pedophile, would want to stay with him and only make him go to therapy? What the heck was therapy going to do? He was a habitual offender who had never gotten caught. And I had been locked up all my teenage years because of his disgusting infatuation with me.

It was too much for me. My husband just held me and let me cry. My little girl woke up and she climbed her little body up the side of my bed and snuggled close to me. I realized I had too much to lose. If I carried out my revenge, my little girl would lose me. I didn't want her to end up like me. I needed to be there to protect her. That was the night I had to give it to God and let it go. I realized I may never get earthly justice; God would have to take care of it, and He did. Dane was diagnosed with Alzheimer's disease at just fifty years old.

CHAPTER ELEVEN

Forgiveness

I always say my children saved my life. I mean that in the most humble way. I had my first child at twenty-one, and I went on to have five more children. People ask me all the time how I do it when they can barely handle one child. I believe God knew it would take six of them to sit me down. I refuse to let them go through what I went through. I refuse to leave them stranded. And I refuse to be a bad example for them.

After that night with Barbara and my sister, I realized I had a lot of emotional baggage I needed to let go. I realized if I didn't let it go, I would harbor anger and fear which would be transferred to my children. By holding on to the anger, I realized I was still letting Barbara and Dane win; I was still letting them have control of me. As a result, after years of not wanting therapy or medication, I decided to get help. I first started with my relationship with God. I had been so blessed, even in the midst of adversity, I couldn't help but give God credit for bringing me through. He always sent people across my path right in my time of need.

I spent years trying to find the right therapist, get on the right medication, and get my diagnosis right. Because of my experience with the mental health field while I was in foster care, I learned how to advocate for myself. I took time to educate myself on different diagnoses and medications to make sure I was getting the help I needed and not the help they wanted me to have.

To this day, I still go to therapy—by choice. I believe therapy is exercise for the mind and is something you should never stop pursuing. However, therapy only works if you find the right match. You can't go to just any therapist and think you'll get positive results. You must be real with yourself, forgive yourself, and allow yourself to be human to truly work through the process. Unfortunately, there is such a negative stigma connected with therapy, but it has been a blessing to me.

Through therapy, I have been able to forgive so many people, including myself, Dane, Barbara, my sister, my biological mother, my biological father, Lester, and any other person who let me down. I found strength in forgiveness. I realized I was not giving them permission to hurt me, but I was releasing them to free myself. They were no longer relevant to my story; they had no more power over me. After forgiving them, the next thing I learned was to pray for them. I learned to let my big Father upstairs handle my battles instead of me handling them. I learned to pray, not to fight.

Forgiveness is not an easy road. It's easier to just stay angry. It's easier to push everyone away so you don't get hurt. It's easier to be the bully. However, forgiveness is rewarding. From forgiveness comes growth, healthy relationships, love, wisdom, and peace. I never knew what peace looked like until I had forgiven those who hurt me. I was so used to drama and dysfunction, life became boring when things in my life were quiet and calm. I would subconsciously self-sabotage and cause things to happen because I didn't trust peace. Today, I view life differently, and I love my peace. There is nothing I won't let go of to keep it.

Finally, I forgave myself for being a participant with Dane. I forgave myself for bullying my sister. I forgave myself for not being enough for my mother to get her stuff together. And I forgave myself for being human. Today, I'm stronger because I forgave myself. That is one of the reasons I decided to write this book. I forgave myself for all the embarrassing things I've done, the men I've slept with, the streets I hung out in, and all the crazy things I've done, because now I'm free from them! No one can hurt me with something I have been forgiven of. I now realize all the things I've been through were not in vain. God has allowed me to turn those things around and help others who have gone through the same things or even worse. Forgiveness is one of the best lessons I've ever learned.

CHAPTER TWELVE

Parents for Parents

When I learned about forgiveness, I thought that was it. I thought I would learn to forgive everyone who had ever hurt me, even if they weren't apologetic, and I would be free. I thought I could literally say, "I forgive you," and start with a clean slate without having to work through any damage they may have caused. I was wrong; forgiveness is a process which takes time and effort. However, I knew if I mastered forgiveness, I would have the answer to a peaceful, fulfilled life. I knew I could rely on God to bring me through, and He did by creating and gifting me with my very own family. I was blessed with the responsibility of guiding my six beautiful children: Auriel, Joziah, Lilliana, Prince, Saint, and Prophecy.

Auriel is my oldest. Her name was derived from the male version of "Auriol," which means "messenger of god." God gave her name to me when she was in the womb, the same way He gave me the names of all my children. Her father and I had her christened at six weeks old, and our pastor at the time prophesied over her and told us she would be a peacekeeper. That prophecy has been true for her up until this day. There have been several times in her little life when she has boldly stood between arguing family members and held her little hands up and said, "We are supposed to love each other. Stop fighting." God has used her so many times. The way her mind works is amazing. "Auri," as we affectionately call her, is a sweet girl. She cares about everyone and does for others and makes them happy. She is super smart too; she wants to know how everything works.

Wherever I take her, she always asks a ton of questions. I love the inquisitiveness she has— all my children have this trait. I like to think that came from me. She is a creator, and can create with anything. She loves to make beats, write songs, or do anything art-related. And she has so many business ideas. I know she will be an entrepreneur one day. She is my first baby! I learned so much by being her mother; I made a lot of mistakes too. However, when I see who she is, who all my children are and the anointing on them, I feel like I haven't done half-bad. Auriel has taught me how to speak kindly because she's such a sensitive person in a good way. She has taught me to see the beauty in everyone and everything.

When Auriel was born, I was just starting a new relationship with God. I wanted to do everything right, and I put pressure on myself to be perfect. To that end, I wanted to get married. I decided to marry Auriel's father when she was six months old. Her father and I went on to have two more children together, Joziah and Lilliana.

I was too young-minded to ask God about getting married, or to ask myself if I was ready. *"Was I wife material? Did I love myself? Did I even know what love was?"* I was twenty-one years old and her father, Robert Munford, was thirty-one. Robert, or "Rock" as I called him, was a hard-working man. He was quiet and a loner, but everyone loved him—so did I! He was my first real love, my first relationship, my first child's father. I was obsessed, and yes, in the crazy kind of way. He was ten years my senior and I was very child-like around him.

I look back now and think he must have really loved me because, baby, I was a hot, spoiled mess! I really loved Rock for Rock and he knew that. However, Rock and I were not good as a married couple. Rock had a temper and couldn't deal with a lot of talking; I also had a temper and talked a lot when I was mad. We could be very toxic together at times. Coming from broken families, neither one of us knew what healthy love was; we were better as friends. Although Rock and I had three children together, we ended up divorcing in 2014.

Our relationship had become extremely toxic. We were both verbally and physically abusive to each other. I was young and didn't see reconciliation in the near future for us. I decided I wanted something healthier for my kids and filed for divorce. However, he remained my friend, my support—my Rock. Unfortunately, Rock passed away in 2018. His death really changed me. I lost my best friend. I didn't have anyone to run to anymore, but in that season, God showed me how strong I could be. I used to ask God why he would let me love Rock, then take him away. Now I understand Rock was put in my life for a season to teach me important life lessons which I carry with me today.

Joziah is my second born, and my first boy. I named him Joziah after the youngest king in the Bible, Josiah. Of course, I had to be unique and switch the "s" for a "z." Joziah is my first wild child; he has absolutely no fear. He is a loner like his father at times, but other times he's super affectionate. He can take apart and rebuild almost anything. Sometimes I think he's too smart for his own good. I swear he should be an attorney when he grows up. He has a legitimate argument for everything, and he is extremely analytical; the way his brain works blows my mind. Joziah is very protective of me; he absolutely loves his mom. All my children do! Joziah has taught me compassion, patience, and understanding. He has even challenged my thought process about how God works. Joziah has moments where he wants to talk about God, and he brings messages to me that make me rethink everything. He has taught me to seek answers from God.

My third child is Lilliana. While pregnant with her, I couldn't come up with a name, so I searched all the baby boards to find the perfect one. I came across the name "Lilliana" and I just knew that was it. Her name means "beauty, innocence, and purity." It is a fitting name because she loves everything beautiful. She has loved fashion since she was two years old. She has this amazing ability to put clothes together and make them work. She loves makeup and all things girly. Lilliana is bold and speaks her mind—she is the little version of me. She is funny, kind (sometimes), and an absolute social butterfly. Lilliana has challenged me to grow; she shows me a reflection of myself and sometimes makes me re-evaluate how I can be better. One of the most affectionate kids I know, she has taught me how to show affection. Lilliana has taught me how to be a lady.

The father of my last three children is Russell Vanwroten. We met at work one year after my divorce. He was a supervisor of a non-profit organization for the homeless, and I was one of the supervisors-in-training of the security company which secured the shelter. I didn't even look his way at first. However, he would bring me breakfast every morning, so I finally decided to give him a chance. Things progressed very quickly and within a month of dating, I was pregnant with Prince. Russell was twenty-six years my senior. At the time I hadn't realized I had a pattern of dating older men—a sign of my unresolved "daddy issues." Unfortunately, I didn't take the time to get to know him; I was swept off my feet the moment I started talking to him.

I was so desperate for love and for my children to have a father. I didn't care what came with it. He was amazing to my kids and he loved them as his own. However, I experienced unimaginable humiliation and pain in our five-year relationship, things I'm still trying to recover from. I spent the majority of our relationship hiding the hurt and our toxic behaviors from my kids. My relationship with Russell ended when he relapsed after being twelve years clean from crack cocaine. I hung on for a little while, but I eventually realized I was losing myself trying to save him from himself. I don't regret the experience, though. I am stronger because of it and I learned a lot about myself.

Prince is my fourth child. I didn't pick his first name, his father Russell did. I wanted to name him "Ezekiel." We compromised and made Ezekiel his middle name. Prince means "royalty," and Ezekiel means "God's strength." Prince is gentle; he is an absolute lover and got me through a lot of hard times when he was born. I called him my human teddy bear. The first year of his life I was depressed, and I would cuddle with him all the time. He has always brought me comfort, even to this day, with his little hugs and random declarations of, "Mommy, I love you." I learned to be gentle from Prince and that it's okay not to be strong all the time. He reminds me not to take life so seriously. He always finds humor in everything, and is pretty funny himself. Prince has taught me how to love.

Saint is my fifth child. He is affectionately called "Sour Patch Kid" by those who love him. He is all boy! Saint means "holy person." Saint is strong, energetic, bold, and completely his own person. He is naturally strong; the boy does a perfect squat effortlessly. He is strong-willed and has been the most resistant child I have, but I love his strong spirit. I know once his spirit it is cultivated, he will be a powerful man. Saint has definitely taken my patience to a new level. However, he has made me a better parent. Saint has taught me that being yourself is more than enough. People will still love you for being your true, authentic self. Saint has taught me self-confidence.

My sixth child—and surprise baby—is Prophecy. After five children, I had gotten rid of all my baby stuff, then here she comes. Her name means, "a foretelling from God." I felt when God gave me her name he was showing me no matter what happened, she would arrive here safely. No one agreed with her name, but I just knew I had to name her that, so I did. I was going through some of the worst parts of my relationship with Russell during my pregnancy. The amount of stress I was under could have caused me to miscarry, yet she remained. Both of us almost died right before she was born. She was born nine weeks early, via emergency C-section, and only weighed three pounds. Prophecy spent the first twenty-eight days of her life in the neonatal intensive care unit (NICU). Today she is a bouncy, sassy, and strong-willed little girl. She is so smart and does not have any developmental delay. She has taught me about God's promises; no matter the circumstance, if God wants it to happen, it will happen. Doctors cannot determine what His will is. Prophecy is my miracle baby.

God made sure I would not be alone anymore. He made sure even when I didn't love myself enough to do what was right, I had six of my favorite people to make me stay in line. I have come to understand that my parents—no matter how many sets I had been given—were part of my journey. They may not have been adequate, but they taught me lessons I have learned from. I have finally come to peace with the realization that I didn't have a loving, close family. I understand there were different circumstances and situations which may have interfered with building a relationship with them. I have honestly grown to be okay with that.

When my sixth child Prophecy was born, I was a single mom at the time, and I had to go back to work, which meant I had to enroll her in daycare. Her caretaker at the daycare was an older lady with a really sweet spirit. I was terrified to leave my baby, but I didn't have a choice. I would drop her off every day with a smile because I didn't want anyone to see I was worried. When I dropped Prophecy off, a lady named Cheryl Allmond would engage me in conversation. Our first conversation was about my daughter's name. She wanted to know why I named her "Prophecy." Cheryl she told me she was a Christian, and that for some reason, she was really drawn to my daughter. I explained to her God had given me her name and she was intrigued.

For the next couple of months after that first day, we would talk every morning, and she learned a little bit more about me. She eventually took time to go to the daycare and get to know each one of my kids. I remember the day she told me I didn't have to buy diapers for Prophecy anymore and I cried. I wasn't used to people helping me. Soon after that, she invited me over her house for dinner. What I didn't know was, during the couple of months she had known me, she had been talking to her husband about me.

After dinner that first night, I received a text message from her asking how I would feel if they adopted me. Cheryl and her husband had been unable to have children and wanted to adopt me as their daughter. I was terrified. So many thoughts ran through my mind. *"Were they trying to take my kids? Was this a game to them? Could I trust them? They might let me down like everyone else. What were their motives? Why would they want me? I came with six kids and baggage."*

I remained scared and distrusted them for a whole year, but they stuck with me, even when I tried to run away from love. Even when I was hard to love. Even when I would throw temper tantrums. On my good days and my bad days—I was just so terrified to love. Accepting their love meant they could let me down, but they stuck with me just like Sam did. One day I woke up and realized they truly loved me. I realized I had done all this forgiving of others, but I still didn't love myself. I still didn't think I was worthy of love. I couldn't believe somebody could love me with all my imperfections. I couldn't believe someone would love me, with all the responsibilities that came with me.

Slowly, I started to learn to love myself, and I began to let them love me. It was a difficult process. We fought, we cried, we laughed, and we grew closer. They had to learn how to be parents and grandparents. I had to learn how to be a daughter and respect authority. It was and still is a difficult adjustment for me. I realized I had so much anger towards men, so I never surrendered. I wouldn't back down, even on the little things. But my dad was so patient with me. There were times he could have given up or called me out of my name or hurt me, but he never did. They both showed me true, unconditional love. They didn't owe me anything and I was a handful. Eventually I realized I wasn't "crazy" as I had been labeled. I was only doing what I knew. My parents showed me a different way and I began to change. They continued to love on me as I was growing, never judging me. I am who I am today because of their love. I'd like to think I've made them proud.

About a year after they initially asked to adopt me, I planned a surprise dinner for them to present them with adoption papers. I had planned the dinner for about a month. I hired a decorator to lay out my backyard, a videographer to capture the moment, and a private chef. I told them we were going to take pictures, which wasn't a lie. I asked them to dress up all fancy and meet me at my house. When they showed up, they were in complete shock. Along with the special meal and photoshoot, I had their family and friends send videos to congratulate them. It was a special night, and they deserved it. They had asked about making the adoption official for quite some time.

At first I got cold feet. I didn't want them or anyone else to think I was doing it to get anything from them. I wanted them to know I genuinely loved them. They insisted the adoption was what they wanted, so I got out of my own way, because I had almost blocked my blessing.

Adoption day came and my parents cried like I was a newborn baby. We made it official January 2021. At thirty years old, I have parents. I didn't think I needed parents, but God knew just what I needed. I was already a mom, what more could I learn? I gave my kids all the love I never had. People always told me I was a great mom. I felt like if I kept strong and kept us together, my children wouldn't need anyone else. Boy, was I wrong. My parents have been the missing element I needed in my life. My father is the first man in my life, other than my grandfather, who never tried to do anything sexual with me. My father has taught me what true love looks like, along with what dedication and patience truly are. He's taught me what a provider looks like, and he has taught me how to set the standard for any man who comes into my life. My father protects me and respects me no matter how difficult I may be.

My mother is meek and mild and has taught me to pray. She has taught me how to respect men. She has shown me how to carry trouble with class and poise, and how to keep myself up as a woman. I'm grateful she taught me how to cry out to God for my needs instead of looking to people. We live in a society in which if you don't have parents, you just get over it and move on. We don't let just anybody come in and be family to us because we don't trust people. I thank God every day for giving me the willingness to give them an opportunity to be a part of my life. I have become a better woman, a better mother, and a better lover because of it. Even parents need parents, no matter how old they are.

CHAPTER THIRTEEN

What Now?

Although I have a very traumatic past behind me, my life is just beginning. I'm thirty years old and finally coming into myself. Most importantly, I have found God again. I grew up around all types of religions, but I strayed away for a long time. It took a bad night in my car for me to decide I was tired of living in The World. The World had not returned the love I had given it. I realized only God could fill the void in my life. I had tried to fill the void with weed, men, friends, shopping, and money; I had tried just about everything. Nothing made my life better and I was tired of trying to figure it out, and I surrendered. I rededicated myself to God in a dark parking lot in Southside, Richmond.

When the trauma in my life died down and I learned how to stop hurting myself, I learned to forgive. I got a chance to actually know myself, not just know all the stuff I've been through, but know the me underneath all of it. Things like what my character is, what I like and don't like, and what I want to do with my life. During the battles of my life, I never had time to say anything about those things. I was always worried about where I was going to live, how was going to eat, if my marriage was going to work, how to get through divorce, or how to be in a relationship with a drug addict. I didn't really have time to think about the basics. However, I stayed true and followed the process, and eventually life calmed down. I surrounded myself with positive people, and God sent support systems for me beyond my understanding. I've done a lot of work on myself, and I'm sure I will continue working on myself. It's just how life goes; every step we grow and evolve. If we are living right, each circumstance, situation, or person we encounter will teach us a new lesson.

Every day we should strive to be better, and to approach each opportunity as a learning experience. After all, this is what life is about, new learning experiences. You make mistakes and you learn from them and you keep moving. When we mess up, we learn, and we don't keep repeating the same mistakes. After all I've been through, I want to help others now. I want to reach those who are in the middle of their crisis and feel like there's no way out. I want them to know no matter how dark their crisis, there is a rainbow on the other side. The rainbow may not show up within days or months or even years, but that doesn't mean it is not there.

There is always hope, even in the worst situations. Wherever you are, that's where you are supposed to be. What you're going through is just a part of your story, and God will use it to help others. It is not a waste of time to do the right thing or to be good to people, even when it seems like everyone else around you is winning although they're doing wrong. What you put out into the universe absolutely comes back to you in time. Your story—your pain—is not in vain. It is going to be used for something good. Your story is already written. God has not forgotten nor forsaken you. The greater the battle you face, the bigger the blessing you will receive.

I have decided my life's mission is to pour into people to motivate and inspire them. God allowed me to go through what I went through because I am strong. Others might not have been able to survive what I went through and still be a good person. God doesn't put more on us than we can individually bear. I believe God allowed me to endure the pain for a purpose. I am no longer angry at Him because I see my purpose. I don't regret a single thing I've experienced, because it all built who I am today. And I am a hell of a mother, a hell of a woman, a hell of a friend, and more than anything, a woman of God.

If just one moment of my past had been changed or altered, I may not be who I am today. If my birth mother had raised me, I may not be who I am today. My story happened exactly the way it was supposed to happen. I am proud of who I am today. I know my story is going to help someone who feels desperate or lonely, someone who believes they should give up, because they feel no one cares about them anyway. But someone does care—I care! God cares! And today you need to start caring. Get up off the floor, dust your feet off, pick your chin up, and God will do the rest of the work. He will send the people. He will send the wisdom. He will send the love. You just have to have the understanding and the willingness to receive.

At his point, I am just enjoying this ride called life—the ups and the downs. I wake up each day with the intention of asking God to lead me. He already knows the plan, so I don't have to figure it out. I fail some days, and some days I revert to my former self. Some days are amazing, and I feel like I got it right. I hurt myself some days, and some days I hurt others. But God gives me a new day every day to get it right again. I challenge you to look over your life and ask yourself, *"What now?"* What are you going to do with the pain and trauma *you* have experienced? Are you going to lie down and let it defeat you, or are you ready to get up and battle? The choice is up to you.

For Speaking Engagements, Book Signings, Appearances, and Interviews:

Contact:
kyla.allmond@gmail.com

Facebook: Kyla Allmond
Instagram: kyla_allmond_